RAGDALE
A HISTORY AND GUIDE

RAGDALE
A HISTORY AND GUIDE

Alice Hayes and Susan Moon

Published by
Open Books
Berkeley, California
and
The Ragdale Foundation
Lake Forest, Illinois

Layout and production by Muriel Underwood, Chicago
Printing by Thomson-Shore, Dexter, Michigan
Published with the help of a grant from The Graham Foundation

Published by Open Books
Berkeley, California
            and
The Ragdale Foundation
1260 N. Green Bay Rd.
Lake Forest, IL 60045
Tel: (312) 234-1063

Copies can be ordered from the Ragdale Foundation.

CONTENTS

♥

PREFACE

♥

Many of the people who come to Ragdale ask me questions, they hear ghosts in the attic, find inscribed books in the bookcases, and wonder about photographs and paintings on the walls. With each generation some of the answers and explanations disappear, and my cousins and I grow older daily, so I've decided to record what we know about the house and its history before it's forgotten. The people who lived in the house were important, because in different ways they gave it its character, and over time the house itself assumed a personality.

I hope this illustrated story will serve as a resource for anyone who loves Ragdale and is curious about its reasons and its makers.

Lots of people have helped in lots of ways to make this book a reality, some of them without even knowing it. I wish to thank all of the photographers, including the people whose photographs we have used and whose names we don't know. I am grateful to the Chicago Historical Society for its care of the Shaw family papers, to Susan Dart and Jack McCutcheon for corrections and additions to the story, to Arthur Miller for his historical perspective and bibliographic knowledge, to Kim Tunney for the spade work she did in her paper, "Ragdale, a Brief History," and to all the members of the Shaw family, both dead and alive, who have contributed stories, memories and information about Ragdale. Thanks to the staff of the Ragdale Foundation, and particularly to

Mike Wilkerson and Sylvia Brown for patiently facilitating our research. Thanks to Muriel Underwood who did the layout and production, to the Graham Foundation for a grant to help publish the book, and to the Ragdale Foundation and the City of Lake Forest for encouraging me to undertake this project. More than to anyone else I am indebted to my daughter, Susan Moon, for her help with the writing, editing and production of this book. She was well suited to this job because she is a writer and editor who has known and loved Ragdale all her life.

I am grateful to my mother, Sylvia Shaw Judson, who gave me the house, to the ancestors, relatives, and ghosts with whom I communed when I came back to live there in 1976, to all the artists and writers who by their creativity have validated the idea of the Ragdale Foundation, and to the many people who have helped to make the Foundation work. Finally, I am grateful to the house itself for its smell and taste and texture and for the views out of its windows and for its nurturing spirit.

Alice Judson Hayes
Ragdale Cabin, 1990

INTRODUCTION

♥

Howard Van Doren Shaw and the
Arts and Crafts Movement

Ragdale, home of Howard Van Doren Shaw and his family, provides both a fascinating insight into American cultural issues of a century ago and also an important perspective on Chicago architecture of that era.

Howard Shaw was born in Chicago on May 7, 1869. His father was a successful dry goods merchant, and the Shaw family lived comfortably in Chicago. Shaw was graduated from Yale in 1890, and then completed an architectural course at the Massachusetts Institute of Technology. He traveled and studied on his own in Europe for a year and a half, sketching buildings wherever he went. He returned home in 1893, and married Frances Wells that same year.[1]

Shaw became a prominent and popular Chicago architect, who designed over 300 buildings, including apartments, churches, factories, the beloved Market Square in Lake Forest, the well-known Lakeside Press in Chicago, and a model town for steel workers in Indiana.[2] Just before his death in 1926, Shaw received

---

1. Susan Dart, *Market Square* (Lake Forest-Lake Bluff Historical Society, 1984), pp. 66-67.
2. Ibid, p. 70.

the prestigious gold medal of the American Institute of Architects, for his services to American architecture. Ragdale, Shaw's country residence in Lake Forest, and one of the first houses he designed, is a fine example of the Arts and Crafts movement, which was at that time establishing itself in Chicago.

The Arts and Crafts Movement had been initiated in England by John Ruskin and William Morris in the final third of the nineteenth century. In 1897, the same year that Ragdale was designed, the Chicago Arts and Crafts Society was founded, and included among its members Frank Lloyd Wright and others who would become known as Prairie School architects. Other important Chicago architects, including Louis Sullivan and Richard Schmidt, who, like Shaw, were members of the Chicago Architectural Club, were also sympathetic to the Arts and Crafts movement.[3] In hindsight, Shaw and Wright appear to represent two extremes of architectural style, but at the time, their shared interest in the new Arts and Crafts movement brought them into the same circle of influential Chicago architects.

Some background on the preoccupations of the age puts Ragdale in historical context. Chicago had been growing at a pace that was spectacular even for an American city. In 1830 it was a wooden fort and a few humble dwellings. In 1871 the city burned to the ground and rose again soon after, such a successful phoenix that by 1890 the population exceeded one million. Immigrants had come in waves, first from New England, and then primarily from Ireland and Germany, to work in the fast-growing industries of the city, such as meatpacking, steel, printing, brewing, and the manufacture of the McCormick reaper. Chicago had become the largest port on the Great Lakes, and the largest railroad center in the world. But by the 1890's, the grown children of the first generation of entrepreneurs were beginning to feel some of the

---

3. Richard Guy Wilson, "Chicago and the International Arts and Crafts Movements," in *Chicago Architecture, 1872-1922*, John Zukowsky, ed. (Chicago and Munich, 1987), p. 212.

Howard Shaw sitting on a bench he made, with two of his grandsons, Jack and Shaw McCutcheon

negative effects of the industrialization that had made them so wealthy, such as mass-produced, sometimes shoddy goods, urban pollution, and a sense of alienation.

In England Ruskin and Morris had been calling the public's attention to the virtues of the Middle Ages, when everything was made by hand. Each household item, each building and even part of a building was idiosyncratic, reflecting prevailing needs and local materials, and marked with the individual style of the craftsman who made it. So, too, in Morris's rural English model, everything was made locally, within the community, with natural and often rough materials like handhewn logs and unbleached wool. Such Arts and Crafts architects as Henry Ives Cobb, Charles Frost, Alfred Granger, Robert Spencer and Howard Shaw based their work on notions of stable Anglo-Saxon culture, on principles which satisfied their longing for order and for respite from rapid change, depersonalization, urban ugliness, and the pressures of new immigrant cultures.

Shaw's Ragdale shows his familiarity with the vocabulary of English Arts and Crafts architecture in the use of the inglenook, the Morris wallpaper, the Cotswold cottage style and roof line, and the timbered stucco. It was built on a comparatively small scale in a rustic setting, a reaction against the grandiose mansions of Lake Shore Drive. The Ragdale lawns and garden, the narrow lanes and the broad vistas, all reflect the traditions of the English romantic and cottage garden, and particularly the influence of Gertrude Jekyll, the eminent English garden designer of the time.

Shaw was not only an architect but a planner, concerned about the community he lived in. Elsewhere in Lake Forest, he designed many country houses, parts of the Lake Forest College campus, and, most notably, Market Square. This English style village square, built in 1916, was the first consciously planned town center in the United States, and an outstanding example of the Arts and Crafts style. The same elements that characterize these later Shaw buildings show their roots in Ragdale: playful ir-

regularity, eclectic architectural imagery drawn from different times and places, a spirit of domestic tranquillity and community, use of natural materials in contrast to the emerging use of steel, and decoration created by individual craftsmen.

Ragdale was designed to be a home, a center of family life, where different generations lived together, and where work was integrated with other daily activities. The living room served as library, music room, study, refuge and hearth. In this room Shaw's father led evening prayers, and here Shaw set up the desk he designed for himself, so that he could work on his drawings surrounded by his family, after a day spent in the impersonal and competitive world of the Loop.

To the north of the house, Shaw built an outdoor theater which he called Ragdale Ring, where plays written by his wife,

Frances Shaw, were performed. Ragdale Ring brought together the various arts of drama, poetry, dance, gardening, set design, and even, in the case of the programs, fine printing. The Arts and Crafts sensibility placed a high value on locally generated entertainment and culture.

One of the unique features of Ragdale is its unbroken continuity as a center for art and creativity. It has been, without interruption, the home of artists. The Shaw family has included two architects, a painter, two poets, a sculptor, a cartoonist, and a weaver, and now the tradition is carried on by the writers and artists in residence at the Ragdale Foundation. Just as Harriet Monroe, founding editor of *Poetry Magazine*, Carl Sandburg, and other figures of the Chicago literary renaissance visited early in the century, so today important and promising writers and artists come for brief stays, to work, and sometimes to perform, and they, too, become part of the extended Ragdale family.

Ragdale is an example of an Arts and Crafts ideal—a suburban ideal, in fact—of a creative life lived in harmonious natural surroundings, in the country, yet within easy reach of the city and its cultural and economic resources. Here at Ragdale one is almost convinced that it is possible to have one's cake and eat it too. A major architect's own home, built early in his career and tinkered with continuously, Ragdale is a laboratory for experiments on survival strategies for family and community life. Ragdale stands today, an ideal still; a challenge to architects, town planners and creative individuals. It calls out for a life focused on human needs for individuality, creativity, beauty, simplicity, and harmony with nature.

Arthur Miller
Lake Forest College, 1990

RAGDALE FAMILY TREE

Theodore A. Shaw (1836-1906) m. Sarah Van Doren (1845-1918)

Howard Van Doren Shaw (1869-1926)
m.
Frances Wells (1872-1937)

Frances Theodora Shaw (1912-)
m.
John Lord King (1909-1966)

Pamela King (1936-)
John Lord King Jr. (1938-)
David King (1941-)

Sylvia Shaw (1897-1978)
m.
[1] Clay Judson (1892-1960)

[2] Sidney Haskins (1893-)

Alice Clay Judson (1922-)
Clay Judson Jr. (1926-1975)

m. [1] Edward Ryerson (1918-)
   [2] Albert McHarg Hayes (1909-)

Evelyn Shaw (1893-1977)
m.
John T. McCutcheon (1870-1949)

John T. McCutcheon Jr. (1918-)
Shaw McCutcheon (1921-)
George Barr McCutcheon (1927-)

CAST OF CHARACTERS

Sarah Van Doren Shaw, 1845-1918, Howard Shaw's mother, a painter and traveler. She spent every other summer at Ragdale, and traveled in the alternate summers.

Theodore A. Shaw, 1836-1906, Howard Shaw's father, drygoods merchant, strict Presbyterian.

Howard Van Doren Shaw, 1869-1926, architect. He designed and built Ragdale for his parents and his own young family to use as a summer residence.

Frances Wells Shaw, 1872-1937, Howard Shaw's wife, a poet, writer, and traveler. She lived at Ragdale six months of the year, while her three children were growing up.

Evelyn Shaw McCutcheon, 1894-1977, Howard Shaw's oldest daughter, devoted wife and mother. She had three sons and ten grandchildren. For the last forty years of her life she lived in a house built by her on the Ragdale property.

John T. McCutcheon, 1870-1949, Evelyn's husband, well-known cartoonist for the *Chicago Tribune*, traveler and adventurer. He was a friend and contemporary of Howard Shaw, and met his future wife Evelyn when she was still a young child.

Sylvia Shaw Judson, 1897-1978, Howard Shaw's second daughter, an accomplished sculptor, especially of garden statues and commissioned work for public places. She was the mother of two children, and lived at Ragdale for many years, longer than anybody else in the family.

18

Clay Judson, 1892-1960, Sylvia's first husband, a lawyer, and lover of wildlife. Although he came to Ragdale by marriage, he and Ragdale took to each other, and it became not only his residence for many years, but his beloved home.

Sidney Haskins, 1893- , Sylvia's second husband, an English Quaker. Although they were married late in life, as widow and widower, Sidney, too, became a part of the Ragdale family. It was he who built the woodshop next to the garage for his cabinetmaking work.

Theodora Shaw King, 1912- , third daughter of Howard Shaw, fifteen years younger than her nearest sister, Sylvia. A traveler and a weaver. She and her husband lived in the Barnhouse with their three children for the first several years of their marriage.

John Lord King, 1909-1966, Theo King's architect husband. He designed Evelyn's house, Sylvia's meadow studio, and the renovation of the barn for his own family.

19

Alice Judson Ryerson Hayes,
1922- , daughter of Sylvia and
Clay Judson, granddaughter of
Howard and Frances Shaw,
poet and writer. She spent
many summers of her life at
Ragdale, then in 1976 returned
there to live for ten years. She
has four children and eight
grandchildren. She started the
Ragdale Foundation and was its
Director for many years. She is
also responsible for making the
arrangements with the City of
Lake Forest and the Open
Lands Association for guardian-
ship and conservation of the
property.

Albert McHarg Hayes, 1909- ,
Alice's second husband, married to her at Ragdale in 1981.
He lived first in the house and
then in the log cabin, and he
has lovingly cared for Ragdale
gardens.

THE CREATION OF AN
ARTS AND CRAFTS HOUSE

♥

Only an hour's drive from downtown Chicago, on Green Bay Road in Lake Forest, stand two wooden gateposts. On one of them hangs a wrought iron lantern which says "RAGDALE." If you enter this gate, you find yourself in a surprising piece of the past. A pair of friendly stone lambs stand in a grass circle in front of a peaceful house. The hearts on the attic shutters give the same welcome they did almost a hundred years ago, and country lanes lead back into the turkey foot grass of the prairie.

Ragdale was built by Howard Van Doren Shaw in 1897, for his parents and for his own young family. He was twenty-eight years old and just beginning his architectural career in Chicago. In 1893 he had married Frances Wells, and by the time Ragdale was built they had a three-year-old daughter, Evelyn, and a brand new baby, Sylvia. Shaw wanted a place to take his family for the summer that was within easy reach of his office in Chicago. What is now the Northwestern Railroad had been built in 1855, and it stopped in the center of Lake Forest, making the trip to the city quick and convenient.

Shaw's father, Theodore Shaw, was the prosperous owner of a dry goods business, and he offered to help pay for the building of a house, since Howard Shaw's still new architectural practice wasn't yet able to support such an enterprise. So, with two friends, Dr. William E. Casselberry and Dr. Nathan S. Davis, Shaw began to look for a rural retreat. The three men found 53 acres of land

21

Front of house, 1902

Back of house, 1900

Front of house, 1965

Back of house, ca. 1950

Front of house, 1978

Back of house, 1970

on Green Bay Road for an asking price of $10,000. Howard Shaw later recalled to his daughter Evelyn:

> I came out to see it, and I said I'd pay a third if they would go along. They agreed. Then it developed we all wanted the wooded corner on the north. I suggested that the one who got the best piece would get the least acreage, and we would draw lots. But Dr. Casselberry said he wouldn't go into it unless he could have the wooded corner piece. So we said OK, and Dr. Davis and I agreed to draw. Then I said, "Well, which piece do you want?" He said he preferred the piece with the rest of the woods. So I said, "Well, I'm satisfied with the larger acreage and some old apple trees." One cold November day I brought out $10,000 in currency, and Swanton, the seller, signed the deed. He lived on the corner of Deerpath and Green Bay. He used to come down and lean on the fence and weep to think he'd sold us the property so cheap.

The piece Shaw acquired had on it an old farmhouse and a barn. Not long after, he bought some additional acreage beyond the Skokie, bringing his total acreage up to 50, at an average of $125 an acre.

The farm property Shaw bought was bare of trees except for an old apple orchard, two honey-locusts in front of the house site, and hickories beside and behind. As I write this, the locusts east of the house and the hickory to the west still flourish. The apple trees that you can see now, even the gnarled old ones, are replacements of the originals. All the other big trees were planted by Shaw or by his daughter, Sylvia. His elms grew to giants, they arched and met over the roof of the house, and then they died of the Dutch Elm Plague. A few big ones remain to the west, but the house itself is again bare of elms. Shaw planted the silver poplars that lean over Green Bay Road, in order to gain privacy from "the dear public."

Green Bay Road runs along a glacial ridge that was one of the earlier shorelines of Lake Michigan. In this flat country it forms a small hill sloping off to the west. Shaw took advantage of this slight elevation to set his house high with a long view to the west. When the foundation was dug, a number of arrowheads were found, mislaid by the Indians who used the ridge of Green Bay Road as a high dry trail from northern Illinois to Green Bay in Wisconsin. When Shaw bought the property, there was an old German woman living on a neighboring farm who remembered seeing the Indians.

Ragdale was Shaw's first chance to build exactly the kind of house he liked best, because it was for his own family. No clients demanded marble hallways or sculptured ceilings. Although his parents paid for the house and shared its use with him until their deaths, they made no demands or preconditions. Howard Shaw could do what he wanted. It cost $5,000 to build the house, and another $1,700 to fix up the farmhouse and rebuild the barn.

As to the actual sharing of the house, Shaw's mother, Sarah Van Doren Shaw, preferred to travel, but she came to Ragdale because her husband liked it, and it was a good place to paint. Their compromise was that they spent every other summer at Ragdale, and every other summer traveling abroad, coming home with cow bells and camel bells. There were travelers in every generation of this family, and the artifacts from all over the world that can still be seen around the house attest to this.

Howard Shaw's own family actually spent six months of the year at Ragdale, and this meant that his older daughters, Evelyn and Sylvia, attended various Lake Forest Schools for part of every spring and fall, and went to school in Chicago in the winter. As a result, Evelyn had South American history seven times, and never once had North American history. Howard and Frances were casual about their children's early schooling.

AROUND THE OUTSIDE
OF THE HOUSE

♥

The front of the house

When you turn from Green Bay Road into the driveway, between the wooden gateposts, the house you see is almost exactly as it was in 1897. The plump doric columns and the inset porch are Shaw trademarks. The wooden beams of the porch and the double peak of the roof suggest English Cotswold architecture. The two big glazed green pots at either end of the porch have been there from the beginning, though they no longer contain clipped oleander trees standing like lollipops. The Shaw-designed bench on the front porch has also been there from the start, as has the ship's lantern by the front door, which now holds a light bulb instead of a large candle. The hearts that are cut out of the attic shutters are the decorative motif Shaw chose for this house he so loved. The hearts reappear in the long bench on the south porch and in the ends of the inglenook benches beside the living room fireplace.

In Europe in the Middle Ages a stone mason often incised his mark into the stones he cut for a cathedral or a castle. At Ragdale, if you look closely, you'll see the mason's marks Shaw personally chiselled into some of the stone slabs of the front porch. There are some of these marks on the south porch and in the garden too: ×'s and +'s and o's.

All the trim, including the window boxes, shutters, window

Two little girls and MacNeill's "Sun Vow" ca. 1917

frames and front door, is painted a particular blue, a color beloved of Howard Shaw and the Arts and Crafts movement. It is a color somewhere between a robin's egg, which has a lot of blue in it, and corroded copper, which has a lot of green—a subtle color that's not available on the paint market but can be achieved by mixing a commercial blue-green with small amounts of gray. The walls of the house are the warm white of Cotswold stucco. The roof is made of gray slate shingles.

The statue that first stood in the circle in front of the house was the "Sun Vow," by Herman MacNeill, now at the Art Institute of Chicago. Shaw's parents saw McNeill modeling it in Rome in 1900, and were much taken with it. McNeill used Indians from Buffalo Bill's show as models. When the Shaws saw the finished statue on exhibit in this country, they bought it. Next, a stone "girl with squirrel" took the Sun Vow's place for a while, then a boy with arms akimbo, and now there is a pair of granite lambs. All three of these statues were made by Sylvia Shaw Judson, Howard Shaw's daughter.

There is an old mounting block to the left of the front porch from which several generations climbed onto their horses.

The copper weathervane of Pegasus, by Max Kahn, on the peak of the roof, was added in 1977, soon after the Ragdale Foundation began.

The house has an informal unpretentious country face: two full stories, with attic windows above, two roof peaks, and salmon-colored geraniums in the window boxes. The knocker on the big front door says "Ragdale." The glass panes of the door are covered inside by a linen curtain embroidered by Frances Shaw, Howard Shaw's wife. It says "Ragdale" again—Shaw wanted people to know where they were.

Every Fourth of July an enormous flag was hung from the second story windows. It reached to the ground and covered much of the porch. When it turned up in the attic recently, it was found to have forty-five stars among the moth holes. In the early days

Max Kahn's "Pegasus" weathervane

Fourth of July

at Ragdale, the Fourth was celebrated by sending up big hot air balloons made of bright-colored paper. The celebrants heated the air by burning excelsior (wood shavings) soaked in kerosene, and they attached notes with their address, and funny pictures. Then they watched the balloons rise and drift majestically off across the prairie. Silently. Fire crackers came a few years later.

The south side of the house

When you walk around the end of the house to the left, or south, you see the open south porch, the fountain, and St. Martin's Glade, a vista carefully created to please a viewer at the

Fountain

Chinese bell on south porch

living room window. This open porch has a high slate roof supported by rough-cut timbers one foot square and now nearly black with age. Between two of these posts hangs a huge Chinese bronze bell with no clapper. But it makes a big boom if you strike it with a padded stick. Shaw probably brought this back from China in 1918. The bench with the cut-out hearts was made by Shaw himself. Under the seat is a compartment for tools and toys and equipment for the fountain.

When his daughters were small, Shaw bought hundreds of cedar paving blocks from the City of Chicago. The city used them to pave its streets, laying them end-up to form a practically indestructible road surface, easy on the feet of horses. The Ragdale blocks, each about one foot long and shaped like a very large brick, were stacked along the walls of the south porch for children to build with. There were so many that a round tower could be built right up to the high porch roof. And the tower could have a spiral staircase going up inside its walls, and slits for pouring boiling oil on hostile marauders. Other structures were built, too, of course. Four generations of children used these blocks. For many years they were put away in the basement in the winter—a chore involving three children, one to hand a block to another who threw it through the open basement window to a third. Then the blocks were carefully stacked for the winter. They lasted for almost ninety years. Tough blocks!

On the porch is a small cast stone figure of "Summer" from a group called the "Four Seasons," by Sylvia Shaw Judson. Below the steps is a cement slab with handprints. When the house was about to be given to the city of Lake Forest, all my children and grandchildren came for a farewell family gathering, and left their marks in the wet cement.

Three fish decorate the stone basin of the fountain. Water sprays from their open mouths. When he designed it, Shaw asked his wife, Frances, who was a poet, to find suitable lines to have carved around the basin between the fish. She gave him these:

PURLING FOUNTAIN COOL AND GRAY
TINKLING MUSIC IN THY SPRAY
SINGING OF A SUMMER'S DAY.

Only after these lines were carved in the stone did Frances tell her husband she had written them herself. Shaw had assumed they were by an English Romantic poet, not by his own romantic wife. For many summers Frances Shaw sat on her second floor porch above the fountain and listened to it splash and purl. At the base of the fountain is the date, "AD 1905," and "H.S."— Shaw liked to sign his work.

Since Ragdale never had a swimming pool, the fountain often

34

Kathryn Nocerino

Above: Fountain basin

*Right: Sylvia Shaw
Judson's "Summer"*

Susan Moon

St. Martin

served that purpose for children, and on very hot days even grownups used to sit in it and read.

Saint Martin, the patron saint of innocent conviviality, sits on his horse on a pedestal in the center of "St. Martin's Glade," surrounded by lilacs and wild roses. In an old apple tree beside him, there used to be a treehouse. Shaw bought St. Martin in an antique shop in France before World War I. He told his daughter, Evelyn, the following story about the statue:

We arranged with the American Express Company to ship it and have it insured. It arrived in twelve pieces. When we claimed our insurance, they said it was not insured against breakage. "What was it insured against? Measles?" I asked. It seems that maritime insurance covers only loss at sea . . .

Saint Martin was a Roman officer . . . He was riding out, one cold winter morning, when a beggar at the gate asked alms. He had no gold, so he took his sword and cut his cloak in half, giving one part to the beggar, who proved to be Our Lord in disguise.

The statue is made of soft French limestone which, although it is covered every winter to keep the frost out, disintegrates in this climate of extremes—hot and cold, wet and dry. By the time you read this, St. Martin may be only a heap of dust.

The back of the house

When you walk to the back and stand far enough away to see the whole house, it looks much bigger—a sprawling comfortable mass of porches and grapevines, with its little hill sloping down to the bowling green at the bottom. Originally, there were old apple trees behind the house, and a hickory. That was all. You could see all the way to the horizon across meadow, prairie and farms.

Gradually Shaw's landscaping behind the house took shape. He decided to make a bowling green, and bought great mahogany bowling balls in England. He encountered a gardener working on a perfect lawn outside an English country house, and asked him how to make a lawn so green and thick and smooth for bowling. The gardener replied: "It be easy, sir. You seed it and roll it and cut it and water it and seed it and roll it and cut it and water it for nine hundred years, and yours will look just like this." So Shaw came home with his bowling balls and bravely began. The bowling

Sylvia and "Sister Bill"

green he created was also used for many summer evening games of croquet.

He wanted a lawn tennis court as well, so he dug a pit about twenty feet deep and the length and breadth of a tennis court, beyond the bowling green. It had to be a sunken court so that it wouldn't spoil the view west from the house. Grass was planted there, white lines were painted on the grass, a net was installed, and his daughters and their friends, in long white tennis dresses with their hair tied back in bows, descended into the pit to play tennis. But because of the slope of the land and the height of the water table they often found themselves ankle deep in mud and mush. So the tennis court was abandoned. Years later, a drier court was built at the east end of the orchard, where the parking lot is now.

The deep pit remained until about 1930. When the family sat on the back porch looking at the view, they ignored the pit. In the late twenties, when Frances Shaw gave up her electric car, she wanted to put it down in the sunken tennis court for her grandchildren to use as a playhouse. It was a sweet and homey little electric car with built-in flower vases and soft plush seats, but the plan was vetoed by the rest of the family. A few years later the deep pit was filled in.

For a while there was a thick, high barberry hedge along the west side of the bowling green. It was so thick that my cousin and I, with a pair of clippers, were able to make a large and prickly cave in the west side of it before anyone noticed. This eventually killed the hedge, and now there is a stone wall in its place.

Originally, the west side of the house had an open porch where the dining porch is now. There was no room or porch above and the original kitchen didn't extend as far west as it does now. These additions were made in 1907, ten years after the house was built, and they gave the house much of the rambling appearance it has

today. If you look from the west, you can see seven porches: one glass, one open, and five with screens. This was truly a house built to be cool in summer.

The north side of the house

At the north end of the house a section of basement was made into a garage in the forties. The tool shed and shop building was added by Sidney Haskins when he married Sylvia Judson in 1963. He made all the benches for the Lake Forest Friends' Meeting in that shop. During the years he lived at Ragdale, Sydney Haskins built benches for the lanes, repaired fences, planned the garden and kept the accounts. He was a conscientious repairer of all kinds of broken things. The shop was his personal domain from 1963 to 1976.

Susan Moon

Tile picture on living room porch

INSIDE THE HOUSE

♥

The front hall

All the woodwork in the front hall is unpainted oak. Originally it was much darker, but Sylvia had it bleached, to lighten the interior. The front hall makes a good introduction to the spirit of

Front hall, 1900

the house, with its curved barrel-vaulted ceiling, and wooden benches under the front windows. All is informal and functional, with loving attention given to detail. Between the hall and dining room are six panels of leaded glass windows, each in a different pattern. Under the windows separating the hall from the dining room are the "candlestick shelves." When the house was built, there were gas lights on the first floor but none on the second, so everyone carried a candle to light the way to bed. Electricity was put in in 1907, but long after that, Frances Shaw still used to say, "It's time to turn up the lights."

On the walls of the hall are trophies brought back from a trip to Italy. The stern panel of an ancient gondola hangs over the living room doorway, and a panel from a 19th century Sicilian donkey cart between the front windows shows a lively scene of crusaders spearing various things.

43

Dining room, 1900

The dining room

In the dining room, the Arts and Crafts style is carried out
more completely than anywhere else in the house. The raised
fireplace has unusually tall andirons designed by Shaw. The
French plates on the plate rack are 19th-century Quimper ware.
The table was designed by Shaw for his Chicago apartment at
1130 Lake Shore Drive, as was the sideboard. Howard and
Frances Shaw's initials appear in the design on the table legs and
a poem by Carl Sandburg referring to this table hangs on the
dining room wall.

The bronze bust of Howard Shaw on the sideboard was done
by his daughter, Sylvia, in the early twenties, a few years before he

Dining room, 1986

died. The original William Morris wallpaper is long gone, and the pineapple paper is a later substitute, but the clock on the mantel and the plates beside it appear in the earliest photographs of the room. The clock worked well until it was electrified along with the rest of the house. There used to be a window seat in the bay. The trim and the beams in the ceiling are painted blue-green.

The dining porch

The dining porch was added in 1909. The curious trellis on its north wall creates a garden-like feel to the room. The deer skulls mounted in flowery garlands were found by Howard and Frances Shaw on a camping trip in Canada. The Indians had hung the skulls in trees as a sign of a good hunting ground. The 17th-century English pub sign on the east wall says,

I am your friend you plainly fee
No harm there can be found in me
My mafter he confines me here
becaufe I knows he sell good beer.

The huge urn with the grape-leaf design came from an Italian vineyard. The archaeological exhibit is of objects found in the prairie: the tines of a great pitchfork, a huge pulley, a piece of

Dining porch, 1986

tackle from a wagon harness, and a fragment from the rim of a giant enamel bathtub, found beside the Skokie. (Could the Romans have been here too?) Also on display is the old T-shaped key for turning on the fountain.

The green table and chairs now on the dining porch were originally in the dining room. Fidgety children and guests used to fiddle with the table drawers and pull them out, so Frances Shaw wrote, "curiosity killed the cat" inside each drawer.

The living room

In the early summers at Ragdale, Theodore Shaw, Howard's father, used to lead family prayers every evening before the children took their candles upstairs to bed. Sylvia remembered how they all knelt in front of the straight square mission furniture and listened to her grandfather, with his long white beard, praying long Presbyterian prayers. Except for a comfortable overstuffed sofa, the living room chairs were straight.

On the porch door frame the heights of children were marked annually. The earliest mark still visible is for a small "JTMcJr-1920" (John T. McCutcheon, Jr., Howard Shaw's first grandchild). The last is for a descendent who was two feet high in 1980. The clock has been on the mantel since 1897. The children used to sit cosily on the inglenook benches by the fire and read, or listen to the reading aloud which was the chief family entertainment. There was always a corn popper hanging by the fireplace and a poker with a sharp point for toasting marshmallows. In storms, the Ragdale banshee wailed in the shutters of the west window. Long-stemmed clay pipes hung below the mantel, and an iron hook in the fireplace held an iron teakettle, for atmosphere, not use. There have always been nature and gardening books on the inglenook shelf, weaving the indoors and outdoors together.

Living room, 1900

Paul Whiting

Living room, 1970

Southeast corner of living room, with Howard Shaw's desk, 1900

In the beginning, instead of paneling, there was a Morris wallpaper covered with a pattern of huge blue morning glories. There were valances at the top of the windows, and printed on the fabric was an Arts and Crafts design of geese walking in a row. A desk Shaw designed for his own use stood against the wall in the southeast corner. It was made of oak, with storage space for long rolls of architectural plans, a place to prop a drawing board, and niches made to fit figures brought from Egypt and Germany. In "Growing Up at Ragdale," Evelyn recalls that her father used to draw here while her mother read Scott and Dickens and Trollope aloud to the assembled family. "And to think they pay me for doing this!" Shaw would mutter.

At first, the northeast corner of the room was walled off and used as a bicycle shed, which opened to the outside, but soon it was transformed into an alcove for a piano. Properly brought up daughters had to have piano lessons, but Shaw never could stand the look of a piano, so a curtain closed it off from the living room. This was also a player piano, so even if you never had piano lesson, you could put on a roll and pump out music. It remained behind its curtain until another generation of unmusical children had come to love *Daisy Daisy, After the Ball was Over,* and the Fire Music from *Siegfried.* They also learned to "compose" by cutting holes in a roll of shelf paper and putting it on a pianola roll. The results were astonishing.

In 1942, Sylvia took out the piano alcove and lined the walls with bookcases instead.

Shaw designed the brass lamps at the ends of the sofa, and Sylvia made the chickens under them during World War II, a time when she and Clay Judson, her husband, kept chickens in the chicken house and sheep in the meadow.

Susan Moon

Frances Shaw reading aloud to Sylvia and Evelyn

This room was filled with a succession of objects brought from far journeys: over the door, a wooden phoenix from China rising out of complicated flames; on the window ledge, a wooden saint with his hands fallen off; and stained glass medallions hanging in the windows.

The framed bookplates beside the door were designed by Shaw for his mother and his two older daughters. This was a family reading room most of all, but the drawers of the tables were always full of games.

The painting of geese on the south wall is by Sarah Van Doren Shaw, and shows the pond that used to be where the garden is now. The portrait of Theodore Shaw reading the newspaper is also by Sarah Van Doren Shaw.

The screened porch to the west is usually cool—a good place to lie in the hammock and read or look out through a frame of grape leaves at the sunset and the view.

The kitchen

By 1909, the big country kitchen was finished. In the corner pantry by the northeast window, great pans of fresh milk from the barn used to stand with the cream rising. The milk pans were passed from the back porch through the pantry window, but the iceman, with his leather jacket and tongs, had to tramp through the kitchen to reach the ice box. There must have been a wood stove at first, but the chimney which still goes through the kitchen hasn't been used for years. The sugar and flour table, with its pull-out bins, still stands against the west wall.

When there was company, the children ate in the kitchen at the big center table. There was a cook, and a maid to help her, and the food was rich and delicious. Fresh vegetables from the garden, fresh sweet corn from the field to the west, home-made cottage cheese, and cream to eat with a spoon. Iced chocolate in tall glasses, lemonade with ice clinking in the pitchers, and cookies and puddings and pies. Not all the children liked the fresh milk warm from the barn, especially during wild onion season. I know one who gagged on the little pieces of cream floating at the top of the milk and was much teased because she begged for the milk that came from the milkman instead of the milk that came from the cow.

The big Delft plaques on the kitchen walls were brought back from Holland by Sarah Van Doren Shaw, Howard Shaw's mother.

She was tall and ramrod straight, elegant in her Edwardian clothes. When she traveled, she painted beautiful small watercolors. Some of them still hang in the house: Saigon, the Nile, Yokahama—all done before 1900. She also painted oils of Ragdale and other places, some of which are still on the walls. She used to dress her daughters-in-law and granddaughters in costumes brought from Holland, and make them pose like the women and children of Rembrandt and Vermeer. If she couldn't persuade them to sit for a painting, she'd photograph them in costume and

paint from the photograph. She signed her paintings "SVDS". In an era when women were considered and treated as amateurs, she was a serious and able painter, and her commitment to her art set an example for her son, Howard, and her granddaughter, Sylvia.

Sarah Van Doren Shaw believed that horses and cows should never be put in the same field lest some horrifying miscegenation should occur. Her granddaughter, Sylvia, remembered an occasion when she was standing at a window with her mother and grandmother and they saw a horse mount a cow in the meadow. "I told you so!" said Sarah Van Doren Shaw to her daughter-in-law, and they hurried the child Sylvia away.

In her recollections of growing up at Ragdale, Evelyn wrote:

One season, when the flies were especially bothersome, my grandmother [Sarah Van Doren Shaw], a city girl, had a happy idea. She

Frances Shaw and daughter, Sylvia, posing on Ragdale front porch, in Dutch costumes brought back from Holland by SVDS

Painting by Sarah Van Doren Shaw

sewed up denim pyjamas to protect the cows, pulling up one part over the forelegs and tying it around their necks, and the back half over the hind legs, fastening it around their stomachs. This proved OK with the cows, but had an unfortunate result. It happened that Dr. Casselberry had a new horse, an iron-grey Arabian stallion called Denmark, who was very skittish. Finally Dr. Casselberry got up his nerve to ride and started down the Green Bay Road toward Ragdale. Coming abreast of the costumed cows beyond the dusty fence, Denmark bolted and dumped the doctor into the ditch beneath the silver poplars near the corner of Laurel. The doctor managed to remount, and rode right up onto the Ragdale front porch, and rang the doorbell in a towering rage. I did not hear what he said to my grandmother.

Sarah Van Doren Shaw insisted that children sit up straight in her tall straight dining room chairs, and she used to tell them, "Always get up from the table hungry."

Upstairs

On the second floor there are five bedrooms, a study, three screened sleeping porches, and four bathrooms, all of them now used by residents of the Ragdale Foundation. The room at the top of the stairs, originally the nursery, has a window seat, and both it and the back bedroom at the west end of the house have sloping timbered ceilings. There is a fireplace in the back bedroom, and the chimney shaft above the mantel is decorated with painted plaster bas-relief designs of leaves and flowers. The upstairs porches are pleasant places to sleep on hot summer nights, and exciting places to be during nighttime summer thunderstorms.

All the paintings in the upstairs hall are by Sarah Van Doren Shaw, except for the small full-length portrait of her which was painted by Martha S. Baker in 1898, just after Ragdale was built, and the portrait of Frances Shaw.

Upstairs bedroom, 1900

In the attic

If you open a certain door in the second floor hallway, you are greeted with a delicious musty smell, and the steep steep stairs to the attic. On rainy days the attic was the perfect place to play, with its sloping roofs and treasures of all kinds under the eaves: a doll's house, a rocking horse, trunks full of old letters, a cedar closet with fancy old dresses, a bookcase full of ancient children's books, and costume trunks galore. It was hard to keep children out of the attic even on sunny days, when they were supposed to be out in the fresh air. Sometimes Frances Shaw wrote at the writing table which still stands in an alcove with windows overlooking the prairie.

THE LANDSCAPE

♥

The lanes, river and meadow

Howard Shaw named his new country house "Ragdale" after an old Tudor house in Leicestershire, England, more because he liked the name itself than because the house was one of his favorites. To him, Ragdale meant meadows and woods and hollow apple trees and country vistas. The raggedy look of the shrubbery, the low hanging branches of trees, and the invasion of the lawn by violets were all deliberate effects. He was aiming for informal country surroundings for his house, not a well-groomed estate.

But the casual setting was carefully planned. Shaw made lanes along both the north and south borders of the property and through the woods, making a total length of about a mile and a half. They were originally intended as a place for the children to ride horseback, but they soon became beloved walkways. They were designed to look like 18th-century English country lanes— sun-dappled tunnels, grassy and narrow, between green walls of native shrubbery planted by nature or by Shaw. At the east end of the south lane he put the Crossways sign, a midwestern version of an English crossroads (as in "ride a cock horse to Banbury Cross"). This was built and dedicated in 1916, in the middle of World War I. The two sand-cast panels at the base were done by Sylvia, who was then 19. One panel shows Indians on the warpath with an angry mask before them, and the other shows a scene of

The lane

Left:
The Crossways,
showing "Peace"
panel

Below: Dedication
of the Crossways,
1916

61

peaceful Indian life with a smiling mask: War and Peace. The arms of the sign point to "Fort Dearborn" (Chicago), "St. Martin's Glade," and "The Skokie."

Family dogs were buried by the crossroads, but the only real tombstone was for Tuppence Ha'penny, Evelyn's fox terrier, who was "chewed up" by a new dog down the road. This gravestone served as the monument for many later dogs and reads:

> HERE LIES
> TUPPENCE HA'PENNY
> FOX TERRIER - DIED MAY
> THIRTIETH 1909 FOR SEVEN
> YEARS LOYAL AND BELOVED

In "Growing Up at Ragdale," Evelyn recalls that her dog died just as she was leaving for the city to take a Latin entrance exam for college, and "the passage to be translated was: 'On the death of his best friend.' I could barely see through the tears."

The south lane runs straight for nearly half a mile, all the way to the concrete bridge which Shaw himself built across the Skokie. In 1897 the Skokie was a shallow stream meandering through water meadows. There was pasture on both sides, and a small oak woods at the north corner of the property. Cottonwoods grew here and there, and across the stream there was a scattering of oak and hickory.

Shaw made a path in the shape of a figure 8 through the woods beyond the Skokie. He built a dam across the stream to form a pond 40 feet wide and three or four feet deep, between the low meadows. People called this enterprise "Shaw's Folly." At Christmas time, Howard and Frances and the two girls sometimes took the train out from Chicago for the day and walked to the pond to skate. The house itself was unheated and unused in the winter, until 1942.

Shaw made rafts for the children to pole on this pond in the

Pirates on the Skokie, ca. 1905

Shaw Bridge over the Skokie

summer, and pennants for the rafts, with skulls and crossbones; and he built a fragile and long-gone little bridge near where the swinging bridge is now.

In 1927, the Skokie was dredged to aid in drainage, and the little bridge, the dam, and the pirate pond were destroyed. The banks of the stream were piled high on the sides to form a ditch. Fortunately, after a few years, this was replaced by a proper underground sewer, and the Skokie returned to being a creek with relatively clean water, but it was never again to be a wide stream meandering through water meadows.

In the early 1900's a railroad line was built near the Skokie, and Shaw was forced to sell a right of way through the west end of his property. Hobos used to camp in the woods, by the train tracks, and Evelyn recalls that "they were always very civil, and careful about their fires." Route 41 was built much later, and the toll road last of all. As late as 1940 it was still possible to ride horseback across the train tracks and all the way west to the Des Plaines River. Many riders used the Onwentsia bridle path, which passed through Ragdale's fenced field where cows and horses grazed (Sarah Van Doren Shaw's beliefs notwithstanding). This made it necessary to have special gates which could be opened and closed from the back of a horse. By one gate John T. McCutcheon, Evelyn's cartoonist husband, painted a sign saying, "Cows and horses reside within. Please close this gate." On the other side a sign declared, "If you're thinking of leaving this gate open, please Don't." This was because the Ragdale cows liked to get into the neighbor's corn and eat it just as it got ripe for the neighbor's table. This did not promote friendly relations.

Shaw built the mold for the cement fenceposts, and he and the farmer and the farmer's son cast and set the more than 100 posts surrounding the field. After the posts were set, Shaw located a farmer with a load of hard-to-find split rails for sale. He paid him generously and went home to send the wagon for the wood. But to Shaw's horror the farmer, out of gratitude for the unexpected

Howard Shaw's split-rail fencing

sale, had sawed all the fence rails into fireplace logs, thinking to save Shaw the trouble. Shaw later found the heavy half-round cedar rails he needed at a sawmill in Wisconsin.

The north lane led back from the woods past a single oak tree. When you lay under it on a blanket, it was like lying on the deck of a schooner in the middle of the ocean, with the grass making waves around you. There was nothing to see but the tree and the open sky. Frances Shaw used to take her grandchildren there to picnic at what she called "the top of the world." Further east on the north lane an oak tree grows in the pathway. It was left there, out of line though it was, because it grew from an acorn planted by Evelyn when she was a small child, probably in about 1905, when her father was planting maples along that part of the lane. Still further east was a stile for the Shaw children to go over to play with the neighbor children to the north. This made a way for children to cross the fence without a gate to forget to close. The ruins of the stile are still there.

Wogden

At the east end of the north lane is a tiny stucco cottage with an arched passageway beneath it. Shaw built this cottage for his wife to use as a writing studio, and he called it "Wogden." The family was fond of silly nicknames—a common habit in the late Victorian era. For some reason Shaw called his wife "Wog," and this was her den. Thus, Wogden. It was built to look like an Irish country cottage, this being the time of the great Irish literary revival. Yeats and Synge were being read for the first time. *Poetry Magazine* was publishing Yeats and other Irish writers' works.

Frances Shaw wrote children's stories, and many of her poems appeared in the early issues of *Poetry Magazine*, and were later collected in a book. The title poem, "Who Loves the Rain," has been frequently anthologized.

Frances Shaw's studio, "Wogden".

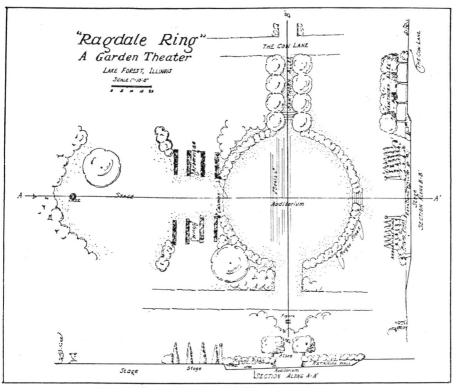

Howard Shaw's design for Ragdale Ring

Ragdale Ring

Frances Shaw was also a playwright, and may have identified with the Irish playwright, Lady Gregory. Her plays were performed by friends and children in the outdoor theater, Ragdale Ring, which Shaw built, in 1912, next to her den. Her plays had titles like: "The Pasha's Garden," and "The Heir of Manville Grange."

Audiences of over 200 sat on benches designed by Shaw. Carl Sandburg and Vachel Lindsay were friends of the Shaws and are said to have come to plays at Ragdale Ring. And Frances Shaw's friend Harriet Monroe, the founding editor of *Poetry Magazine,* may have brought Yeats to Ragdale Ring when he visited her in Chicago. Those were the days of accomplished amateur actors, and Lake Forest boasted the Aldis Playhouse as well as Ragdale Ring. People were willing to go to greater lengths to entertain themselves in the days before movies and TV.

Shaw's design was a copy of an outdoor garden theater he had seen at the Villa Gori, outside of Siena, Italy. The audience sat in a circular orchestra paved with grass and surrounded by a low limestone wall. The stage was at the level of the top of the wall, with evergreens forming wings for entrances and exits. On both sides of the stage stood columns topped with baskets of stone fruit. During a performance, banners or Japanese lanterns were hung around the theater. A stone balustrade behind the theater reached from Wogden to the cow lane, along the edge of a terrace. During the intermission of a play, the audience strolled on this terrace and looked at the view. Shaw installed a sophisticated lighting system: three tiers of floodlights, and two spotlights. He was the lighting director, and operated the lights during the performances.

In an article called "Audiences and the Open Air," Frances Shaw wrote about Ragdale Ring:

> It was my fate to wake up one morning to find myself in full possession of an Out-of-Door Theatre! I had known for several years that something had been going on in the rough pasture north of the cow lane. I had known its name—but somehow I had never realized that a time would come when I was to do anything more about it than sit around with my book, in shady places, and watch my contented husband and architect safely and harmlessly work off his surplus energy, and come hungry to his week-end meals.
>
> Suddenly I was told by the creator of this mechanism that it was ready, and that we must produce, before an audience of some 250 people, something pleasing, original and "not too expensive" . . .

RAGDALE, on the
Green Bay Road
Lake Forest, Ill.

"In the Pasha's Garden"

Will be Given at

Ragdale Ring

Thursday Evening, August 27
(*In case of rain August 28*)

At Half After Eight O'clock

You are invited by Mr. and Mrs. Howard Shaw

*Invitation to Ragdale Ring, 1914, designed
by Howard Shaw*

I found in *The Atlantic Monthly* a little story by H.G. Dwight called "The Pasha's Garden." It had a pretty plot in an oriental setting. There was no dialogue and no ending. But I took the story and used it, and I take more pleasure in thinking of this entertainment than in any we have had. It was gotten up and rehearsed in ten days and the neighbors complained that they could hear the Keeper of the Harem keeping it an acre away.

. . . The whole happy day and night of "The Pasha's Garden" is a perfect memory. The lanterns hung quietly, the forked gonfalons [banners] did not have to have their ends tied down, the incense in the two brass bowls on the stone wall burned steadily. On the long, blue refreshment tables no vases tipped over, no scarves blew up over the baskets of dates and fruits into the Turkish coffee. And the young, orientally-garbed program-passers were happy swinging their feet from the back wall of the Ring. . .

"The Pipes of Pan" in Ragdale Ring, 1914

But sometimes, weather was a problem:

> I will not harrow you with details about the night the little cloud drifted down from Waukegan, and stopped—perhaps from curiosity—among the stars just directly above Ragdale Ring, and emptied its entire contents in a sudden deluge on the august representatives of the Garden Club of America . . .

> I have decided I will write a camping drama, staged about a smoky bonfire, with our cow done up as a buffalo in the background, and on the invitation it will say, "In case of pleasant weather, the play will be postponed until the next stormy night."

After Shaw's death in 1926, no more plays were given in the Ragdale theater. Frances Shaw wrote the following poem as a tribute to her husband and to Ragdale Ring:

In the Theatre

> Early for the play
> The lights are dim,
> Lonely
> In the theatre he built,
> Lonely, I think of him.

> These walls enfold
> His living thought;
> Here dwells the beauty
> That his hand has wrought;
> In every line his heart, his brain;
> Here I am near him
> And he lives again.

As a legacy from the theater, the Ragdale attic was always full of costumes and properties, and dressing up out of the costume

Garden gate

trunks enlivened many a family gathering over the years. Hundreds of Japanese lanterns are still there, although they now fall apart at the slightest touch.

Evelyn McCutcheon, Howard's oldest daughter, built her house (now owned by the Augustin Harts) on the edge of Ragdale Ring in 1936-37. But a large part of the circle and the stage remain, as well as the approach from the garden through the "pleached alley," a tunnel of intertwining hawthorne trees.

The garden

The original garden was close to Green Bay Road, and passersby would steal the vegetables, so it had to be moved. To the northwest of the house a two-track wagon road going down to the meadow passed a pond. Soon after the house was completed Shaw filled in the pond to keep the neighborhood children from falling in. And Evelyn, in "Growing Up at Ragdale," admits she used to push the Casselberry children (whom her father always called "the whortleberries") into it. In this fertile spot Shaw laid out his new garden.

The garden started out twice its present size. It was outlined with small arbor vitae trees—now grown to a great size. They were planted where the garden paths crossed. The garden gateposts remain as they were in Shaw's time, when they formed an entrance to Ragdale Ring. On top of the concrete posts are baskets of flowers, and on either side of the gate stand small Chinese lions. Across the top of the posts is a design in wrought iron, with an "R" for Ragdale in the center.

Along the east border of the garden was a flourishing grape arbor, and every fall the little girls trampled out the vintage with their bare feet. The wellhead in the center of the garden came from

The dovecote

France. There is a real well below, but when water was eventually piped into the garden the well was covered over, in order to prevent children from falling in. To the east of the garden there used to be a well house with a hand pump in it and hearts cut out of its walls. At the west end of the garden is a dovecote, and although it is a faithful copy of an English dovecote, doves could never be persuaded to stay in it. It is flanked by two stone heads on pedestals— one is a mask of tragedy, and the other, though it looks like Socrates, is really a satyr. Socrates never had such pointed ears. The cabin gate was painted by John T. McCutcheon, Ragdale's resident cartoonist. The beds on the side of the garden were originally planted in vegetables and berries. Flowers and apple trees grew in the center.

The sundial, designed by Shaw, has this verse inscribed around it:

Hours Fly
Flowers Die
New Ways
New Days
Pass By
Love Stays

The original garden was cultivated by the farmer who lived in the brick house by the barn, and the Ragdale family was amply supplied with vegetables as well as flowers. Every fall the family pulled an old cider press into the orchard and made apple cider.

In summer, there was a kind of yellow primrose which opened as soon as the sun set. Supper was planned so that it would be

Making cider in the orchard

over in time for everyone to walk down to the garden and stand in a row watching the primroses open. You could actually see them move—a natural movie, with sound effects by a chorus of mosquitoes.

On the way back to the house the family sometimes stopped for a game of croquet, or sat down to watch the afterglow of the sunset over the fields. Then came reading aloud, and then the children were put to bed on the upstairs porches, where they lay on their cots listening to the reassuring squeak of the hammock as the grownups talked quietly on the livingroom porch below.

The barn

When Shaw bought the property, it was a working farm. The brick farmhouse had been built in the late 1830's and is the oldest house still standing in Lake County. In "Annals of Ragdale," Shaw described it as "the most dilapidated thing you ever saw." He made repairs on the farmhouse and built a new barn, cowshed, wagon shed, and shop to form a courtyard adjoining the farmhouse itself. He built a limestone dry wall with a wide wooden gate to form the fourth side of the courtyard. For the cupola above the slate roof, he designed a weathervane with an R for Ragdale.

In the early years, the man who took care of the horses lived in a room off the hayloft. The Shaw horses were not fancy. The team, Rob and Roy, although stylishly named after Sir Walter Scott's novel, was not a matched pair. Rob was a tall bay, Roy was a smaller sorrel. When Shaw's adolescent daughters drove the team to meet their father at the commuter train, they found it humiliating to wait beside their neighbors' splendid carriages, with coachmen, footmen, polished brass lamps, and elegant matched pairs of horses.

The family had a couple of riding horses and a pony, as well. They raised chickens, pigs, and lambs. Two or three cows kept

SCENES AROUND
RAGDALE FARM

*Above: Rob and Roy
and the buggy*

Right: a neighbor

77

Haystacks

Ploughing

The ponycart

them in milk, and heavy farm horses pulled the hay cutting machinery in the field. Rock was the farm horse I remember. Wearing big flat leather overshoes so his hooves wouldn't make holes in the lawn, Rock also pulled a lawn mower.

When the hay wagon came back from the meadow, the children would sometimes ride on top of the load, and then watch it get pitched into the hayloft. This is now the upstairs of the barnhouse. The dusty hayloft was a glorious place to play, and so were the haystacks down in the meadow, where the extra hay was piled. Luckily the barn is still there, even though my cousin and I picked the hayloft as the place to smoke our first forbidden cigarette. And once we caught hundreds of butterflies in the garden, and filled the cupola with their bright fluttering. We were sadly surprised when they all died of the heat within an hour. Other favorite barn activities for children were helping to milk the cows, and pedaling the whetstone in Grandfather Shaw's shop. That shop is now the barnhouse studio.

SECOND GENERATION
AT RAGDALE

♥

Division of property

After Frances Shaw died in 1937, Ragdale was divided between her three daughters.

Evelyn McCutcheon built her house beside Ragdale Ring, with
a view across the prairie to the sunsets she loved. Her husband,
the cartoonist John T. McCutcheon, took over the old cowshed,
added a skylight and a fireplace, and made it into a cartooning
studio and museum to house his trophies from all over the world,
including such things as a gamelan from Bali, a wastebasket made
from an elephant's foot, and Pygmies' poison arrows.

The youngest Shaw daughter, Theo King, and her architect
husband, Jack King, remodeled the barn and joined it to the old
farmhouse to make a rambling house, where they lived with their
three children. The wagon shed became Theo's weaving room. The
courtyard was paved with bricks from the streets of Evanston.

Sylvia and her husband, Clay Judson, used the main house
as a summer residence until 1942, when they winterized it and
moved into it year round. Then Clay Judson took the commuter
train into his law office in Chicago. The changes they made in the
house were minimal. The old coal furnace was replaced by a gas
one, and the plumbing and wiring were renewed. They had bookcases built in the front of the living room. Sylvia removed some of
the small decorative features of the house which seemed to her

Original farmhouse and barn, before King remodeling

self-consciously quaint, like the old Dutch tobacco pipes hanging over the fireplace. But essentially the house was unchanged.

The three sisters jointly maintained the garden, the meadows and the woods. They did what they called "making lane," which meant that grownups and children, armed with clippers and axes and a picnic, would go down to prune and clear the lanes. When Rock, the farm horse, was gone, they bought an International Harvester Cub tractor. When she was eighty, Evelyn still delighted in mowing the meadow with this marvelous spidery antique.

The prairie

Nobody knew there was a precious prairie down beyond the mowed field until the late sixties, when a young botanist, Robin Moran, discovered it. He was still in high school, but he recognized

that this was no ordinary meadow, but a remarkable example of undisturbed prairie. He brought it to the attention of Sylvia, who already knew many of the wildflowers by name. She called in the prairie experts. They found 70 species of prairie flowers. And they found acres of giant blue stem, or turkey foot grass—the same grass that is famous for covering the prairie, horse-neck high, when the early pioneers passed through Illinois. The Shaw prairie is now recognized for its ecological importance, as one of the last remaining sections of virgin prairie in the region.

Later, the City of Lake Forest buried a sewer line down through the middle of the prairie, but otherwise it has been little disturbed. Ironically, a spring of pure water appeared when the sewer-digging cut through an underlying layer of limestone, and up bubbled the pure groundwater from below.

Over the years, ownership of the woods and prairie has been

gradually transferred to the Nature Conservancy and the Lake Forest Open Lands Association. The first gift was made in 1961, and at the time of this writing, the Open Lands Association has come to be the custodian of all the Ragdale property west of the stone wall behind the house, except for the cabin and its lot, and the part of the meadow that was sold with the old McCutcheon property.

The bonfire

From the beginning, the brush that was pruned, cleared, and gathered up from the ground on the nearly fifty acres of Ragdale land was heaped into a big pile in the middle of the first meadow, and burned in an annual bonfire. By 1908, the bonfire had become an institution to which all the children in the neighborhood were invited. There were Scottish bagpipers and marshmallows to toast. Weather permitting, the bonfire took place on the night of the harvest moon. In her later years, Evelyn McCutcheon presided in her golf cart, distributing the marshmallows. For eighty years now, there has been an uninterrupted succession of bonfires. The Open Lands Association now owns the field, gathers the pile, and lights the fire, and they plan to continue the tradition.

The log cabin

In 1934, Chicago's second World's Fair, the Century of Progress, closed. Its buildings were sold, and Sylvia and Clay Judson bought "Abe Lincoln's Indiana Home" for $100, and had it moved to Ragdale. It was an old log cabin that had been brought to the Fair from Indiana, and displayed there as an approximate replica of Lincoln's Indiana cabin. Sylvia was a sculptor, and she worked in her sculpture studio in Chicago in the winter, but she needed

The cabin

a studio to work in during the summers spent at Ragdale. She had part of the cabin loft taken out and a skylight put into the north roof. In order to make it useable as a weekend cabin, an addition was built containing two tiny bedrooms, a kitchen and a bathroom. It so happened that the plumbing from the dressing room of the famous fan dancer, Sally Rand, was also for sale, so Sylvia bought that, too, and for a little over fifty years the fan dancer's shower, toilet and washbasin existed in startling conjunction with Abraham Lincoln's spirit at the Ragdale cabin.

In the 1950's, after Sylvia became a Quaker, the cabin was used briefly as a Meeting House. By then Sylvia had the meadow studio. When the cabin addition had to be replaced in 1986, the plumbing fixtures that could be salvaged were put into the new bathroom, so the spirit of Sally Rand still lingers. The cabin itself sits, essentially unchanged, on the edge of the prairie.

The meadow studio

When Sylvia needed a year-round studio, Jack King, Theo's husband, designed the sculpture studio in the meadow. Here she worked for thirty-five years. Now it is used by resident artists of the Ragdale Foundation. A wooden angel stands high against the south wall of the studio. When Howard Shaw designed the inside of the Fourth Presbyterian Church on North Michigan Avenue in Chicago, he ordered fourteen angels from Italian woodcarvers in New York for the tops of the pillars in the nave. Fifteen were delivered by mistake, and he brought the extra one out to Ragdale, where she (or he?) has become famous as the "extra angel."

During World War II, the family built a sheep shed and a chicken house with Jack King's help as designer. Sylvia and Clay collected the eggs, fed the chickens and delivered the baby lambs

Sylvia Shaw Judson working on her studio porch. The "extra angel" is in right foreground.

in spring. Sylvia's statue of lambs in front of the house was inspired by these wartime lambs in the meadow.

In the 40's, a new generation of Judson and McCutcheon grandchildren played on the bowling green and explored the attic. Reading aloud continued to be the principal evening entertainment, sometimes varied by a game of bird lotto or crochinole.

The Shaw sisters had inherited from their father a passionate concern for the aesthetics of Ragdale. Branches of trees were never pruned without endless consideration of what effect the pruning would have on the view, and yet perfection was carefully avoided, so that the landscape kept its old-fashioned, rough-edged, romantic beauty.

The sheep shed, 1943

Clay Judson feeding the chickens

View west, 1945

THE RAGDALE FOUNDATION

♥

In 1976, I was given the house by my mother, Sylvia, and with her blessing I began the process of turning it into the Ragdale Foundation. For the first few years it remained a family residence for the summer and at Christmas time. Writers were invited to use it during the rest of the year. Some of the family traditions continued into the life of the Foundation: cider making with the old press, eating in the garden, walking on the prairie, cooling one's feet or even one's seat in the fountain on hot days, reading in hammocks on porches, playing croquet, dressing up in clothes from the attic, and following the piper to the bonfire in October. The character of the house itself has survived whatever renewals, repairs and renovations have had to be made over the years.

At first, just three or four writers could be accommodated. My study was the office, and I was cook, secretary and tractor-driver, as well as Director. But in 1980, the barnhouse, which had been sold in the late 40's to the Preston family, was bought back from them by the Ragdale Foundation and adapted to its needs. Howard Shaw's old shop was remodeled into an excellent artist's studio, a big restaurant stove went into the kitchen, and the passageway from the old brick house to the living room was transformed into the Foundation office. These were the visible changes. In the spring of 1981, after the renovation of the barnhouse, the Foundation was able to provide living and working space for seven more writers and artists. Altogether, twelve resi-

Alice Hayes mowing the meadow

dents can now be accomodated at a time. With a staff apartment in the main house and another in the barnhouse, the Foundation has become bigger and more professional.

In the spring of 1986, the City of Lake Forest was entrusted with the ownership of both houses. It accepted the responsibility for the maintenance of the two buildings and the grounds immediately around them, and the following year the garden was added to the City's property. Shaw's Market Square and the architecture of the many big houses he designed were so important to the special character of Lake Forest that the City was eager to have Shaw's own Arts and Crafts style house, now on the National Register of Historic Places. It has been agreed that the Ragdale

Foundation can continue to operate its program in the buildings for at least 25 years. The City has been very considerate of the needs of the Foundation, and the Foundation has shared the public rooms of the Ragdale house with various Lake Forest groups, for meetings, seminars, and other public events. From time to time there is a large open house, so that people from Lake Forest can visit the Ragdale which they now own.

The old laundry in the basement of the house is now the office of the Lake Forest Open Lands Association, which owns almost all of the original Ragdale land. So the prairie and woods and meadow remain permanently connected to the old house, and defended

In costumes from the attic, 1981

from commercial development for a long time to come. Although Ragdale is in a suburb of Chicago, there are deer and foxes, mink, raccoons and possums, and hundreds of species of birds and wildflowers. The house still looks out for a clear half mile across the prairie, just as it did when it was built.

The City of Lake Forest, the Lake Forest Open Lands Association and the Ragdale Foundation are the triple guardians of Ragdale. With their care it should last a long time.

The spirit of the Arts and Crafts movement is expressed in the architecture and landscape of Ragdale, it permeates the house and barn, and it continues to have an intangible but real effect on the creativity of those who work here.

CHILDREN AT RAGDALE

1900

1911

1923

1925, houses made of chairs

1944

1984

1989

IMPORTANT DATES

♥

1897 Property bought in Lake Forest by Howard Shaw
1898 Ragdale house completed
1909 Additions to house
1926 Howard Shaw dies
1934 Lincoln cabin purchased and moved to Ragdale
Property divided among the three daughters
1937 Frances Shaw dies
McCutcheon house begun
1939 King remodeling of Barn begun
1942 Judsons move into Ragdale after winterizing
1943 Meadow studio built
1948 Barnhouse sold to Mrs. Frederick Preston
1961 First gift of land to Nature Conservancy
1976 Gift of Ragdale to Alice Ryerson
Ragdale Foundation incorporated
1980 Barnhouse bought from Henry Preston and adapted for
Foundation use
1986 Foundation ten year celebration
Gift of House and Barnhouse to City of Lake Forest
1987 Sale of last piece of Ragdale land to Lake Forest Open
Lands Association

A PARTIAL BIBLIOGRAPHY

♥

Authors' note: The main source for this book is the long and intimate knowledge of Ragdale shared by its authors. Between us we have a hundred and fourteen years of close association with the house and the family history, and much of what we have written here is information that has been informally handed down from one generation to the next.

Below we have listed several different kinds of bibliographical resources, including: books written by members of the family which are connected in some way with the place itself; published books and articles which contain some information about Ragdale, Howard Van Doren Shaw, or prairie botany; and finally, some manuscript material by family members, and a list of libraries where this material is available.

Arpee, Edward. *Lake Forest, Illinois, History and Reminiscences, 1861-1961,* Lake Forest-Lake Bluff Historical Society, 1979.

Bogue, Margaret Beattie. *Around the Shores of Lake Michigan, a Guide to Historic Sites,* University of Wisconsin Press, 1985.

Bushey, Charles L. and Moran, Robbin C. "Vascular Flora of Shaw Prairie," pp. 427-436, in *Transactions,* Illinois State Academy of Science, Vol. 71, No. 4, 1978.

Dart, Susan. *Evelyn Shaw McCutcheon and Ragdale,* Lake Forest-Lake Bluff Historical Society, 1980.

_____ *Market Square,* Lake Forest-Lake Bluff Historical Society, 1984.

Eaton, Leonard K. *Two Chicago Architects and their Clients: Frank Lloyd Wright and Howard Van Doren Shaw*, Cambridge, Mass., 1969.

Hazen, Judith and Oelz, Jessica. *A Field Guide to the Wildflowers, Shrubs and Trees on the Nature Preserves of the Lake Forest Open Lands Association*, 1989.

Judson, Sylvia Shaw. *The Quiet Eye, Regnery*, 1954.

_____ *For Gardens and Other Places*, Regnery, 1966.

Lowe, David Garrard. "Prairie in Flower," pp. 68-75, *House and Garden*, August, 1989.

McCutcheon, Evelyn Shaw. *Growing Up at Ragdale*, manuscript in Lake Forest College Library.

Moon, Susan. *Post Cards from the Attic*, Open Books, 1982.

_____ *Aunt Marty and Uncle Charlie Go to Giza*, Open Books, 1987.

Popham, Walter D. "Ragdale Ring," pp. 324 ff, *House Beautiful*, March, 1927.

Ryerson, Alice. *New and Selected Poems*, Spoon River. 1987.

_____ *Ragdale Lives*, Ragdale, 1985.

Shaw, Frances Wells. *Plays, Stories, Essays*, Ragdale, 1937.

_____ *Ragdale Book of Verse*, Gothic Press, Lake Forest, 1911.

_____ *Songs of a Baby's Day*, McClurg & Co., Chicago, 1917.

_____ *Who Loves the Rain*, Lakeside Press, 1940.

_____ *Wake Up, Old House*, unpublished children's book about Ragdale, ms. in Lake Forest College Library.

Shaw, Howard Van Doren. *Annals of Ragdale*, as told to Evelyn Shaw McCutcheon, 1922, ms. in Lake Forest College Library.

Sprague, Dr. Paul E. "Estate Development in Lake Forest," extracted in *Lake Forest Preservation Foundation Newsletter*, Fall, 1989.

Tallmadge, Thomas E. "Howard Van Doren Shaw," *Architectural Record* 60, July 1926, pp. 71-73.

Tunney, Kimberly. *Ragdale: A Brief History*, Lake Forest-Lake Bluff Historical Society Docents Training Manual, 1987.

Vosmik, Julie L. *The Early Domestic Architecture of Howard Van Doren Shaw*, M.A. thesis, University of Virginia, 1982.

Wilson, Richard Guy. *The AIA Gold Medal*, New York, 1984, pp. 47-59, 156-157.

Zukowsky, John, editor. *Chicago Architecture, 1872-1922, Birth of a Metropolis*, Chicago and Munich, 1987.

Family Papers at:

Burnham Library, Art Institute of Chicago

Chicago Historical Society

Lake Forest College Library

Newberry Library

100